A True Story About Button

John D. Drenchko

(Bill Knapp's "Uncle Jack"

John (Jack) D. Drenchko

VANTAGE PRESS
New York / Los Angeles / Chicago

To my sister, Terry, who loves all animals and who has devoted so much of her time helping to train, feed, and take care of Button

FIRST EDITION

Published by Vantage Press, Inc.
516 West 34th Street, New York, New York 10001

Manufactured in the United States of America
ISBN: 0-533-07972-1

This is a true story about "Button," a two-year-old, seven-pound lop-eared bunny. He was named by my niece, "because he's cute as a button." His long hair is basically white, but he also has an abundance of brown evenly divided on the sides, back, front and top of the head.

I first saw him in a pet store and fell in love with him. I love all animals and there were other bunnies in the store. But somehow there was something about him that attracted me more than the others. Perhaps it was the way he kept sitting up. I did not buy him right then and there. However, he was on my mind the rest of the day. While trying to fall asleep that night, I came to the conclusion that I must have him. So, the first thing the next day, I brought him home.

(Note: Of course I did not know at this time the surprises Button had in store for us—which led to a write-up about him and his picture on the front page of the local newspaper. More about this later.)

Button was six weeks old and a little frightened when I placed him in a wire enclosure that I had hurriedly put together in the basement. I also made a hut for him, as most animals like to retreat to a hideaway, where they can feel secure from danger, and sleep. However, Button did not seem to care for the hut and preferred to nap on top of it.

After two or three days he not only got over his fright but managed to leap over the enclosure to explore his surroundings. Therefore I enlarged the area of his pen, which was two feet high. During this time he was fed clover, some apple, wheat bread and rabbit pellets. He had a good appetite. It wasn't long, probably another two or three days, before Button escaped the enclosure again. I came to the conclusion he just did not want to be penned up. So he was given the freedom to roam around the basement.

I also made a larger hut for him, thinking perhaps he may have felt cramped in the first hut and for that reason did not care to use it. The new quarters had nice soft padding for him to sleep on. The first thing Button did was rumple up the padding and toss it out the opening with his paws. That convinced me he wasn't partial to huts. But it was left there, for he occasionally napped on top of the hut. Other times he would snooze on a coffee table or daybed in the basement.

Since the basement was large, it was necessary to get Button to use one area for his "bathroom needs." A tray with cat litter was placed in a corner. My sister Terry and I took turns putting Button in the tray.

At first, Button came to the conclusion the litter was placed in the tray for his fun, for he scratched and attempted to dig, scattering the litter in all directions. Since that wasn't going to work, we decided to continue his training, using only newspapers. When one of us placed him in the corner on the papers, we would stand there for a while. It was soon apparent Button was a fast learner and knew what was expected of him. He occasionally had an "accident" elsewhere. We periodically placed him on the papers to make sure the lesson would remain with him. Patience paid off, for after about two weeks Button always used the corner. He was now considered "housebroken."

We decided to bring Button upstairs to the kitchen, where he met Penny, our small brown-and-white Pekinese-Spaniel dog, for the first time. We watched to

"This would make a good hut if it wasn't so cramped."

see how well they took to each other. They smelled each other and it appeared the greeting was more like a "Hi!"

It wasn't long before a mutual fondness for each other began to develop and they would take naps side by side. Penny was a gentle dog. She would not hurt another animal, no matter how small it was, and I believe Button sensed that.

About two years before Button came into our lives, Penny found a tiny baby bunny and dropped it in the grass at the feet of my sister. She picked it up and saw it was still alive. There wasn't a mark on it, attesting to how gentle Penny was. Terry put it on a cloth in a small box and covered it. I arrived about an hour later, and she showed me the baby bunny. Its eyes were not open yet. It takes about nine days for a baby bunny's eyes to open after birth.

We decided to carry the little bunny, Penny following, to where she had dropped it in the grass. We asked Penny to show us where she found it. She seemed to understand and took us further into the garden, where we found another bunny that had crawled away from the nest. We assumed something had happened to the mother rabbit and that she would not be back.

The two tiny bunnies were fed warm water-diluted evaporated milk with an eye dropper several times a day. In two days their eyes opened. In ten or eleven days they began to munch on clover, lettuce, and occasionally a little apple. From time to time, Penny would hover over them as if they were her own offspring.

As they were growing it was obvious, since they were wild bunnies, they wanted to be free. So when I thought they were big enough—about two months old—they were set free to scamper into the garden, from which they began to explore their surroundings. They lived in the area for quite some time.

Now to get back to Button: when he was upstairs in the kitchen we would periodically take him to the basement to his private "bathroom" in the corner. Nights he would spend in the basement, with Penny sometimes going down there to keep him company. We soon learned how intelligent Button was.

Late evenings I would put a little chicken or turkey in a dish for Penny's usual snack. Was I surprised when Button quickly hopped over and began eating. He ate several small pieces and Penny did not seem to mind. After that, whenever I stood at the kitchen counter preparing Penny's snack, Button was there at my feet sitting up and occasionally banging my leg with his front paws for some of that newfound delicacy. That went on for some time, before he tired of the fare. Fowl is not part of a rabbit's usual diet; therefore, I was glad when he went back to his normal menu.

Button was now about three months old. He loved to have someone gently scratch his nose, forehead or ears. He also showed considerable affection. He was now at the age that curiosity takes over. We allowed him in the living room, where he liked to perch on high places. First it was the coffee table, then the couch. That wasn't high enough, so he climbed to the top of the back of the couch. But when he jumped on an easy chair, then onto an adjacent table that held several potted flowers, and pushed one to the floor, that put a damper on his activities in the living room.

Most bunnies, when they are quite young, for some reason like to chew upon things, such as lamp cords. Button chewed up a telephone cord and a TV lead-in line. The solution was to keep them away from him—which sometimes wasn't easy. In time he outgrew the habit.

Whenever we were not in the house, we kept Button in the basement. One day I was outside doing some chores,

"I wonder who that is."

and my sister went next door to visit a neighbor for a few minutes. After a while I came into the house to pick up a tool I thought I had left in the living room. I was surprised to see Button there on the floor taking a nap. I assumed my sister had meant to take him to the basement but had forgotten to do so. When she came back, she assured me she had taken him there before leaving. The question was then—did he climb the stairs on his own? It would be unusual for a bunny to do so. We knew Button was adept, but climbing stairs—no way!

About 11 P.M. I took Button to the basement and left him on the day bed. However, next morning when my sister got up, there was Button in the living room. So there was no question that Button knew how to come upstairs. And it wasn't long before he showed us he could not only go up the stairs at will, but down as well.

We concluded new measures would have to be taken. A removable screen was installed in the doorway separating the kitchen and living room to let him have the use of the kitchen and vestibule at night. For now Button was housebroken and would go to the basement when necessary. After a few days of practicing going up and down the basement stairs, Button was able to come up the steps like an "express train." He came up so fast, he would skid on the linoleum when he tried to put the "brakes" on at the top of the landing. This now opened up a whole new series of adventures for him.

Sometimes when my sister would get up in the morning, she would find Button in the living room despite the fence to keep him out. Watching him, she found he could push the screen aside with his head to gain entrance. It was then necessary to place a stool against the screen. This seemed to work and kept Button from moving it. At night he would sleep on a cushion on a footstool or sometimes on a carpet on the floor.

It was now getting too cold to take Button outside. But since he spent most of his young life indoors up to now, he was quite content scampering upstairs or down to the basement.

In fact he surprised us one day when the attic door was left ajar, and he scooted up the fairly steep stairs to the attic. It was dark there, but he did not seem to mind. He did this two or three times. However, we tried to keep him out of the attic, for it was easy for him to hide among all the boxes and articles stored there. Button usually came when called, but he could be stubborn too.

Since we lived in a ranch house—with kitchen, living room, bathroom and bedrooms all on one floor—it gave Button a greater area to investigate. Sometimes he would leap upon a bed in the spare room to try to get a couple of stuffed animals, a Teddy Bear and Chow Puppy, interested in playing with him. When they would not respond, he would push them aside and take a nap.

Other times he would take naps on an easy chair by a large window in the living room. That was one of his favorite places. When the sun directed its rays upon the arm of the chair, he would stretch out and place his head there. Button had his own chair pad, as occasionally he'd get a notion to scratch at the seat with his paws, before settling down to snooze. From time to time he would find other places to nap, such as on an end table that held a lamp and telephone. He would favor a couple of napping places for a while, then find another. Sometimes he would take a nap with a stuffed bunny that my niece had on another easy chair. Other times Penny and Button would take a nap side by side in the sun on the living room floor. Button had a way of sitting up, which he did frequently, especially if he wanted something or just to greet someone. One day the mailman came into the house

"Hey, Roddy, why don't you come over here?"

to deliver a special piece of mail. Button ran over to him and sat up. The mailman just laughed and thought it was so cute.

Evenings we would watch TV. One evening I was sitting in a special chair I like. Button came into the living room and surprised me by jumping on my lap. It was obvious he wanted company and affection. He settled on my lap facing the television set. I caressed him as he lay there and he seemed to be enjoying it. He would close his eyes, then open them and appeared to be watching TV. However, Button wasn't too comfortable, as his legs kept slipping off my lap. The next day I found a pad which I placed on my lap. That was ideal, for now Button appeared quite comfortable.

From then on it became our evening routine. When I would sit down, Button was there to leap upon my lap. If he did not jump up immediately, he would just look up at me to pick him up. Other times he was there waiting for me, or if I was still in the kitchen reading the paper, he would come over to me, sit up and hit my leg with his paws. That was the signal for me to stop reading and move to the living room.

Sometimes he liked to get up on a stool alongside of me, place his front paws over one leg and lay his head on the other leg. On other occasions he would just nestle in my arms.

During the cold winter months my sister liked to use a small spare bedroom for sewing and writing, because it was warm there. Both Penny and Button loved to take naps there as well. As soon as she entered the room to write or sew, they promptly followed her to find a comfortable spot.

By now Button would respond to his name quite readily. However we also used pet names such as Bo-Bok and Buster, which he would mostly ignore.

There was a long table against the staircase in the basement. Occasionally Button would go down the steps as far as the top of the table and jump on it to investigate the few items there. If something new was placed on the table he would check it out thoroughly. After shopping at the local supermarket, my sister would bring the bags of groceries to the basement and place them onto the table. If Button was there, he would promptly scamper up a few steps onto the table to check out the bags, first peering inside, then scratching at them with his front paws, as if to say "I want to see all that's in there."

If nothing more interested him on the table, he would leap with ease to the floor, then sit up and look around. I think what was going through his mind was "Let me see, should I rumple some carpets, or climb up on something." Those were two of his pastimes.

During the summer, the basement door to the outside was left ajar. I closed it and went upstairs. A half hour or so later I went to look for Button. I could not find him anywhere. I looked behind the easy chairs, couch, under the beds and just about all his usual haunts. I rushed outside fearful he might have gotten out. Uppermost in my mind were the occasional stray dogs that roam around. After a thorough search and no Button, I went back to the basement. On a couple of occasions he had gotten locked in the cold cellar, where canned goods, fruit and other items are kept. However, he wasn't there either.

After another trip upstairs I returned to the basement. All this time I kept calling his name. As I stood there, slowly turning around picking out the places he favored, I finally spotted him perched high on some stacked boxes, looking at me quizzically. I think he was enjoying my frantic search for him. I was so relieved I picked him up and cuddled him, for by now Button was a cherished member of the family.

"How is this pose?"

Button could be quite mischievous and playful. It was not unusual for him to untie my shoestrings. I would retie them and he would promptly untie them again. When he tired of that, he would pull down my socks with his front paws. He also liked to tackle the broom when someone was trying to sweep.

Another time when I was working on a project at a small table against the wall, Button hopped up on the table and proceeded to rumple the stack of newspapers and push them to the floor, using his paws and head. When the papers slid over the side, he slid with them. When he tried to hop back up, he slid off again. I was watching to see what he would do. He looked up and had the situation figured out in a flash. He promptly went to the other side and jumped back up on the remaining stack of papers. Once he had had enough of that, he crossed over to my lap. So I had to stop what I was doing to play with him for a while.

It was now approaching March. Button was a little over six months old and still growing. On reasonably warm days he was allowed outside for a few minutes at a time to get used to the outdoors.

It did not take Button long to learn that a refrigerator contained food. A couple of his favorites were parsley and bananas. When my sister would open the refrigerator door to get some parsley he was right there, his paws on the bottom shelf. He ate the offered greens so fast, it was simply amazing to watch them disappear. Of course, he wasn't allowed to have too much. He loved bananas too and was allowed a small piece each day.

His regular meals consisted of endive, escarole and lettuce for the greens. Clover too, when it was available. He loved apples and pears and was given a little of each every day. Although he was also given carrots, this bunny wasn't fond of them. He also had a fresh supply of alfalfa pellets to munch on. Occasionally he liked to nibble on dry wheat toast. By now the reader must have come to the conclusion that he was being spoiled. I'll have to admit, he was.

On occasion we would spoil him even more, when he would sit up by the table during mealtime, asking for something special. It would either be a piece of berry muffin or apple pie. He loved both, especially the muffin. So when my sister baked muffins, she always set aside a couple for Button.

One day we had apple pie for dessert. I went to the basement to get something. When I got back, Button was on the table eating my pie. He was having a feast. I put him back on the floor and of course gave him some of the pie in his dish. There wasn't too much sugar or salt in the desserts, so we did not mind if he had some occasionally.

Sometimes when I was eating he would sit up for some, too. I would break off a piece and hold it for him to nibble on. He would smell it, and if it wasn't to his liking, he would just rub his chin on the offering and hop away.

Button was as curious as any kitten—perhaps more so. If a large package was brought in and placed on the floor, he promptly jumped on top. He was right there as it was being opened. Even before the contents were all taken out, he leaped inside to investigate further.

If a small kitchen stepladder was brought out to get something from a high cabinet, Button was up on the top step first. Once the back cover of a large floor-model TV was removed to make repairs. I went to the basement to get some tools and—the reader probably guessed it—Button was inside among all the wires when I got back. Of course, the power had been disconnected.

Button about five months old

Button and pal Penny eating lunch

"I'll bet I could mow the grass if the handlebars were put back."

Button takes over the stepladder to rub his chin.

"*Oh, these flowers smell so nice.*"

Button taking a nap with his friends

Perhaps Button is wondering why he receives no response from the lambs to his greeting.

Button's favorite pose

"This clothes basket seems like a nice place for a nap."

"I think I'll take a nap for a while."

There were times when Button liked to nap in a more private place than on an easy chair, footstool, or the floor. He liked to take a nap after his lunch for two or three hours. Some of his favorite spots were on one of the chairs pushed under the kitchen table hidden from view by the tablecloth overhang, behind the TV, or under the bed in the spare bedroom.

By late March Button was approaching seven months old. The basement also leads up a few steps to a breezeway that connects to a workshop and outside. It did not take Button long to follow me into the shop. He was in his glory—a new place to explore and investigate. There were two lawn mowers—one a riding type, a Rototiller, and a lawn roller, besides a long table and numerous odds and ends. Button checked out each in turn and especially liked the riding mower, because he could comfortably perch on the seat and survey his surroundings.

After a little time in the workshop, I opened a side door leading to the garage where two cars are parked. Like a flash Button left the lawn mower seat and hopped into the new area. He began scratching at the cover hanging over one of the cars. He seemed to derive some sort of pleasure out of that, for he did it everytime he was in the garage.

After Button tired of romping in the breezeway, shop and garage, he generally headed for an adjacent flower bed, where he proceeded to dig holes. His favorite place to dig was under the shrubbery in front of the house. While he was having his fun I had to stand close by, for occasionally a stray dog wandered into the vicinity. Not knowing what the dog or Button might do, I just picked Button up and carried him back to the garage.

Eventually I obtained a harness for Button and attached it to Penny's freedomline. The wire stretched from the house to a corner of the garage. A small pully wheel was connected to a nylon cord and the other end to the harness. The wheel rolled freely over the wire and gave him a wide area to roam.

It wasn't long before Button began to object to his limited freedom by chewing at the harness wherever he could reach it. Therefore, it was necessary to replace the nylon cord that made up the harness part from time to time.

Whenever I was working in the garden in the back-yard, I would hook Button's line to one of the clotheslines. There he would romp around the evergreen trees, apple trees, or in the garden. Needless to say he really enjoyed it. Occasionally he would spot a distant "cousin"—a wild bunny who lived under the evergreen trees. Button and the wild bunny would sit up and look at each other for a while and then go about their business, the wild bunny munching clover and Button about as before.

Once Button got outside without our knowing it. A neighbor saw him and came to the house to inform us that he was scampering from place to place. By now he was well-known by the neighbors. I spotted him in the garden and called to him. When he saw me, he ran and jumped into my outstretched arms as I stooped down to gather him to me. I think he had begun to feel lonely and a bit frightened without a familiar face around.

After that scare we were more careful when going out. Button loved to go outside and would quickly sneak through a door, as it was opened—especially if one wasn't looking down.

The first time I took Button for a walk around the house and garage with his harness I thought he would be tired after one trip around. But no—once around wasn't enough. We circled the house three times, and it was I who was beginning to get tired, not Button.

One evening I decided to walk around the house and

The author taking Button for a walk

grounds, Penny on one line and Button on another. I tried to keep them from becoming entangled as we walked. When we got to the front of the house, a lady driving by stopped at the stop sign, glanced over and saw this strange, or perhaps unusual, combination taking a stroll. She just threw up her arms and laughed. I am sure she must have told all her friends and acquaintances of the unusual trio taking a walk.

As the days became warmer, Penny and Button would spend more time outside, napping in the shop or garage with the doors open to let the sun in. Sometimes they would share a carpet and nap together.

Since the weather was now so pleasant, Button wanted to spend more time outside. Each time the kitchen door was about to be opened, he was right there ready to squeeze out. Of course he wasn't permitted out whenever he wished. But an idea came to me. The combination storm and screen door had a solid panel in the lower half. Why not a window, so he could at least look out. A small section was cut out and a suitable window installed. That seemed to Button's liking, for he now spent much of his time by the window gazing outside. He also looked forward to taking a snooze there in the mornings as the sun came streaming in.

Button was also beginning to learn to use the side door leading to the kitchen whenever he wanted to enter the house. When it was time to come in, I would take off his harness and he usually followed me up a few steps of the patio to enter. Sometimes he would dash ahead and wait by the door for me to get there.

When we were walking around the yard, the neighbors' pet dogs would get excited. They would love to have gotten out to romp with Button. When we walked by, however, their barks did not seem to bother Button.

"Button wants to go into the house."

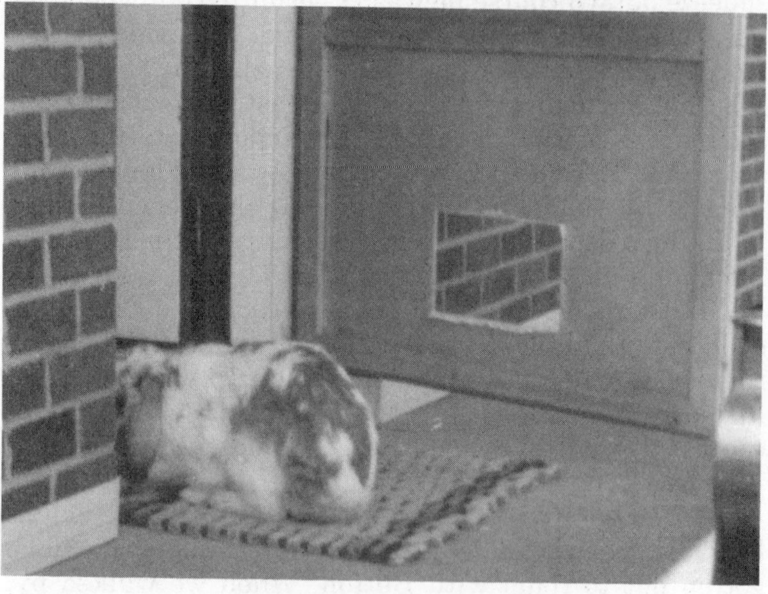

The door (with his lookout window) is held open for Button while he enters.

Button had numerous admirers in the neighborhood. The paper girl would occasionally come over to pet him when she would deliver the papers. Or when he was in the house and she came by to collect for the papers, she never failed to ask "Where's Button?" If he hopped into sight, Rhonda would pet him and remark, "He is so adorable."

Our neighbor's young daughter named Tina loved animals and had a small dog named Princess. Sometimes she played with Button, rubbing his ears, head and nose, which he enjoyed. Princess is a very gentle and quiet dog and very friendly with Penny. When Button would come near the fence, and Princess was on the other side, they would sniff at each other. Of course, Princess got excited but rarely barked.

As I was writing this in longhand Button was next to me on a footstool enjoying the warm sun. I found it quite relaxing sitting in a chair with a board on my lap for a writing desk. I had to stop writing for a while when Button decided he wanted some attention and leaped on my writing board to "check out the story," I presume. He then turned around and reached up to kiss me. So I put my pen and board aside to cuddle him and devoted a few minutes to pampering the little rascal, after which he decided to hop to the floor to stretch out for a nap. As I watched him for a few moments I thought, *He looks like a bunny, but with all his antics, he must be part dog, part kitten and part goat all rolled into one.*

During the early part of May I noticed a wild rabbit had dug a hole under a hydrangea bush in the yard. It must have been done at night. The hole was covered with dry grass. I assumed there were baby bunnies inside.

One day a heavy rain storm was about to break. Fearful the rain would drown the bunnies in the hole, I quickly put a plastic covering on the bush over the area around the hole. The bushes were low enough so that it wasn't too difficult to fasten the covering. It was a terrific storm, and the rain surely would have drowned the bunnies, for there were puddles of water everywhere.

However, I believe the plastic covering scared the mother bunny away, for she did not come back to feed her young. Even though I took the covering away after the storm there was no disturbance of the grass on and around the hole and I knew she had not shown up. I was worried the little ones would starve. The next day, when she still did not make her presence known, I removed the dry grass and peered into the hole. There were the baby bunnies huddled together in the fur the mother rabbit had pulled from her body to make the nest. I got a small box, lined it with soft cloth, and took the bunnies out one at a time. Their eyes were open, so they must have been at least nine days old. There were six of them. I covered them and took them into the house, then made up a formula of warm water and evaporated milk. Using an eye dropper I tried to feed them. But none of them would drink the milk. I was concerned that they would starve, so decided to try again an hour or two later.

In the meantime I went outside to look around and a few minutes later spotted the mother bunny nearby. The baby bunnies were hurriedly placed back in the nest and the hole covered as it was before. I also marked the opening with a tuft of grass, which would tell me if she had fed her babies. However the next day I knew they weren't fed. It is a known fact that once human hands touch the offspring the mother will stay away. Again I brought the bunnies inside and promptly prepared the same milk formula. They certainly must have been half-starved by now, for every one of them eagerly began taking the milk and from then on it was no problem feeding them. They were fed four to five times a day.

Two of the bunnies were quite small compared to the others. Perhaps they had not gotten as much nourishment as the others. It was doubtful they would survive. However as the days went by they seemed stronger and more alert.

After about eight or nine days a little bit of tender clover was placed in the box with them. Some of the bunnies began to nibble at the new food. They were still fed milk, however, but one by one they quit drinking milk and began eating more clover. The first to quit was the smallest one. Clover is an excellent food for bunnies, for it contains a number of vitamins.

It was so delightful to watch God's little creatures romp and scamper about. The box that contained them was fairly tall but soon not high enough. They began jumping out of the box. So a hole was cut out on the side of one end of the box and a screen placed over the hole. The top was then of course covered. Sometimes the bunnies would gather at the screen to peer out and other times huddle together at the other end of the box.

I prepared two boxes, each lined with newspapers and cloth. When one was being cleaned—which was daily—the bunnies were placed in the other. They had good appetites and it was apparent they were rapidly growing.

During all this time Button did not show much curiosity, except when I held one in my hands. He would then sit up and sniff the bunny.

Two weeks after they had been brought into the house, it was evident the six bunnies needed more room. Therefore they were moved to the basement and placed in larger quarters—a wire cage. A small hut was placed at one end, where they could hide and sleep.

Besides clover they were now given some apples and dry bread. They really loved the apples.

From time to time Button would lie beside the cage and watch the bunnies as they scampered about.

It wasn't long after they were moved to their new quarters that a neighbor brought over a small wild bunny he had caught in his tool shed. He was afraid the cat next door might catch him. I placed this new addition with the others. He was the smallest of the group and somewhat shy and would spend most of the time in the hut, coming out only to eat. But after three or four days he began to mingle with the others outside of the hut.

About this time it became obvious some of the bunnies wanted to be free, as they would run from one end of the cage to the other, trying to get out. However, I kept them about two weeks longer to be sure they were able to take care of themselves.

When they were about two and a half months old and perhaps half grown, they were released in a wooded area behind a church about a mile from here. In a way it was sad to see them go, as my sister Terry and I, and I'm sure Button too, enjoyed watching them scampering about.

Our local veterinarian said it was difficult to raise wild baby bunnies and they probably would not survive. Therefore, although it involved considerable work caring for them, we had the satisfaction of knowing that they all survived their captivity.

When outside Button would be left to his own designs without the harness, if someone was close by to keep an eye on his activities. The harness was not to his liking, even though it was light and fit him well. He would just as soon chew it off. One of his favorite places was the workshop, where the lawn mowers and the Rototiller were kept. His favorite perch there was the seat of the riding mower.

One day when he leaped off a toe of his rear foot got

caught momentarily in a hole of a screen shield that covers the transmission between the back wheels. The result was a torn toenail and considerable bleeding. I am sure the pain was excruciating. The first thing Button did was to lick his wound, as animals normally do. We promptly applied medication to prevent infection and promote healing. As long as Button remained more or less stationary, the bleeding stopped. But when he began to hop around, the wound would open and start to bleed again. As he hopped from one place to another, he left a trail of blood. Something had to be done. It wasn't convenient to place an ordinary bandage or a Band-aid on his foot, and it had to be padded to cushion the wounded area.

We then hit upon the idea of a sock. While I kept Button from moving about, my sister went into the house, found some ribbed cloth, and fashioned a suitable sock for him on her sewing machine. The bottom of the sock was padded with cotton, placed over his foot and tied into place above the elbow part, to prevent it from coming off. It fit so well, it looked like part of his foot. The test now— would it prevent the bleeding as he hopped about? After a couple of hours there was no visible indication that the bleeding resumed. We kept checking his foot every hour or so. By evening Button had accepted the new addition as part of his foot and even wet the tip with his tongue and proceeded to wash his ears, as rabbits generally do.

The next day the first thing in the morning we inspected his foot and we found the sock to be free of blood. Later Terry made another sock to replace the one Button had on when it became soiled. It was somewhat humorous watching Button hopping about with a sock on his foot. After four or five days his foot was pretty well healed. When it was taken off, I believe he missed it, for from time to time he would look back at that foot.

Rabbits have delicate digestive systems. Kittens also

have a problem with fur balls in their stomach from swallowing hair when they wash parts of their bodies. The same is true of bunnies. If they itch, they will chew at that part, and hair will accumulate in the digestive system. Consequently they will not eat. This happened to Button on a couple of occasions.

When he was off his feed he would eat very little. A young friend of ours named Joey dropped over for a visit. I asked him to get some greens out of the garden, such as endives, lettuce, parsley and a carrot, to see if he could persuade Button to eat. Joey would get down on his hands and knees and hold each vegetable under his nose, hoping the aroma of the garden goodies would induce him to eat. But to no avail.

The next day I received a magazine on rabbits that I subscribe to. In the periodical was a timely article written by a veterinarian, in response to a request by a girl whose bunny was also having eating problems. To get rid of the hair by dissolving it in the stomach or elsewhere in the digestive tract, he suggested giving the bunny an enzyme, such as that derived from papaya or pineapple.

Button was given papaya on one occasion and pineapple on another. The tablets were crushed and mixed in a formula of pureed greens, apple, carrots, and alfalfa pellets. A syringe was filled with the mixture and a little was fed to him. He appeared to like it. It was more convenient to hold Button on my lap, with a plastic dish on a paper towel to catch any droppings of his food. If I was slow in refilling the syringe, he would pick up the dish with his teeth and toss it on the floor. Soon Button began eating a little more on his own. I still used the syringe to feed him at least once a day. The only problem was he got to like that method too well. Being a softie, I pampered him further and continued to supplement his feeding that way for quite some time.

Button was one year old September 3. By this time Penny, who was approaching eighteen years of age, was beginning to feel poorly. Whenever cats and dogs get that old, as a rule their kidneys begin to fail. By the end of the month Penny had passed away. It was a sad time for all of us, for we loved her dearly. It goes without saying that she truly was a member of the family and will ever be in our hearts.

Having Button around was a blessing, for it helped to fill the void left by the loss of Penny.

It was obvious Button missed her and could not understand where she could be. He searched the rooms looking for her. We felt so sorry for him we bought a stuffed doggie that somewhat resembled Penny. But that did not fool Button. He would hop over to the toy, sniff at it, nudge it with his head, and then hop away. We fussed over Button more than usual to ease the loss of his buddy and companion. In time he seemed to be his normal self again.

During the next few months, Button never ceased to amuse and surprise us with some new antic. He liked to follow us into the cold cellar, where fruits such as apples, oranges and grapefruit were kept in containers on the concrete floor. A favorite pastime of his was to sample the apples and roll the oranges and grapefruit out of the trays and over the floor while one's attention was diverted elsewhere.

The basement was between sixty-seven and seventy degrees Fahrenheit, and the adjacent cold cellar about ten degrees cooler. Now Button was so quick that on more than one occasion, he would slip in there without being seen and get locked in. With the door closed very little light penetrated.

It wasn't long before his absence was noted. After quickly checking his usual haunts, the cold cellar was checked. Sure enough there he would be. On one such

"Did you call me?"

occasion, when the door was opened, there was Button munching on some carob candy balls. He had actually opened a small cardboard box, taken out a sealed plastic packet of the sweets, placed it on the floor, and ripped it open with his claws.

Button usually had three or four favorite places where he liked to rest. On one occasion when my sister was sitting on the couch and cutting some cloth on a low coffee table, Button was at the other end taking a nap. He soon became wide awake and curious as to what she was doing, so he hopped over. Fearful she might injure him with the scissors, she placed him on the floor. But he wasn't to be denied. He went around the coffee table, jumped upon the couch, and made a leap for the table, landing on some magazines. The result was that Button and the magazines slid to the floor. It really was funny to watch. This did not deter him, for he was back on the coffee table in a flash. This time she let him stay, taking extra care not to hurt him with the scissors.

Sometimes we took a walk around the outside of the house without his harness. I led the way and he followed along to the delight of the neighbors and their visitors sitting outside.

Since Button spends a good deal of time outdoors with us, he will occasionally manage to get himself dirty by digging under the shrubbery or hopping around the workshop or under the cars in the garage. This called for a sponge bath, using a baby shampoo. Of course he was never soaked to the skin. The soiled areas were sponged off lightly and then thoroughly wiped dry. He's not too fond of these washings—especially of getting his front paws wet. At one time as the preparation was being made for his "bath" in the basement, he recognized the two small pans, one for clean water and the other containing a shampoo water mixture. Away he went, like a "streak," upstairs!

When Button was about eighteen months old and pretty well known in the neighborhood, I stopped in at the local newspaper office to renew our subscription. A reporter there who had heard about Button asked if she could do a story about him. Of course I was elated. She came to the house the following day with her camera and found him taking a nap in the sun on an easy chair, his head on the arm.

After viewing some of the photos I had taken of him at various stages of his capers and taking notes on some of his activities, we went outside to take more pictures. The one that appeared on the front page of the paper with the story was of Button coming outside as I held the door open for him. Of course, after that Button became something of a celebrity in his own right.

Another summer was coming to a close, and autumn would soon be upon us. This meant Button would be close to his second birthday. I could not help but think back to some of the events since he came to us. During the time this story was being typed up, Button was usually nearby. In fact I placed a chair for him next to mine, where he could snooze while I was typing. Once I left to get more paper. When I got back, there he was, on my chair with his front paws on the keyboard. Perhaps he wanted to add something to the story.

I can't understand how the expression "dumb bunny" came about. I am sure rabbits, like other pets, would show a surprising intelligence if given a chance. Perhaps Button is exceptional, due to our patience in training him. Of course there was much work involved but a certain amount of thought and reasoning must have come from his own brain. How many times we have witnessed Button's capabilities; when blocked one way he would take an alternative method or route. Such intelligence one generally attributes to a human.

When a dog barks or a cat meows we can derive certain messages from the sounds. But with pet bunnies, we have to be content with actions such as a nudge with the head or paws or a leap upon one's lap.

In conclusion, I would like to add that the affection, laughter, and companionship Button has given us were far beyond our expectations.